Let all that you do be done in love.

—I CORINTHIANS 16:14

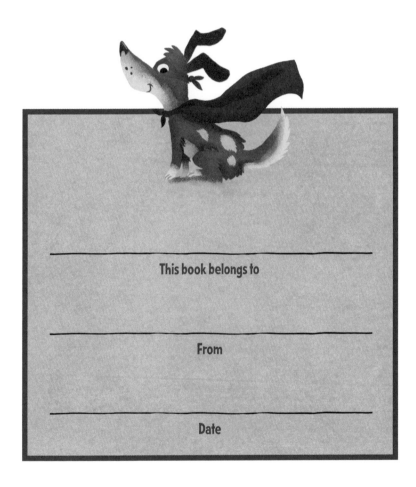

This book belongs to

From

Date

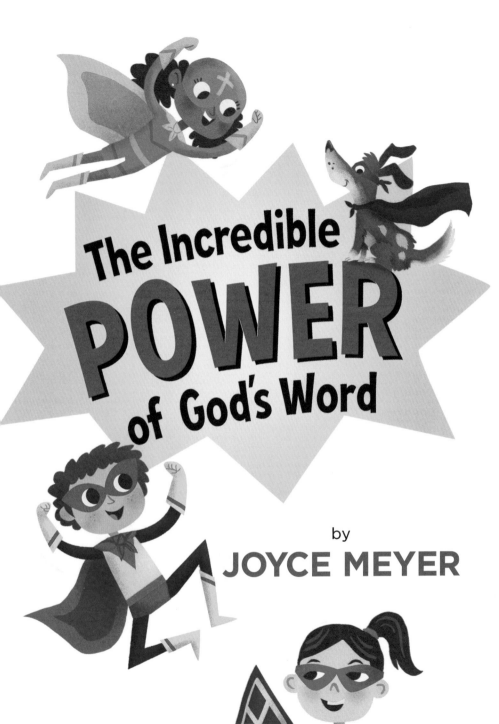

The Incredible POWER of God's Word

by

JOYCE MEYER

ISBN: 978-1-5460-3444-5

WorthyKids
Hachette Book Group
1290 Avenue of the Americas
New York, NY 10104

LCCN: 2020051838

Unless otherwise noted, Scripture quotations are from the ESV® Bible (The Holy Bible, English Standard Version®), copyright © 2001 by Crossway, a publishing ministry of Good News Publishers. Used by permission. All rights reserved. | Scripture quotations marked NIV are from the Holy Bible, New International Version®, NIV® Copyright © 1973, 1978, 1984, 2011 by Biblica, Inc.® Used by permission. | Scripture quotations marked NLT are from the Holy Bible, New Living Translation, copyright © 1996, 2004, 2007, 2013, 2015. Used by permission of Tyndale House Publishers Inc., Carol Stream, Illinois 60188. All rights reserved.

Art by John Joseph
Designed by Melissa Reagan
Interior design by Jeff Jansen | Aesthetic Soup

Printed and bound in China • APS
2 4 6 8 10 9 7 5 3 1

Contents

A Note from Joyce

Did you know that what you're holding in your hands isn't an ordinary book? This little book is filled with God's promises—words that you can speak out loud over your life to help you get to know God and understand Him better each time you open the pages.

Proverbs 7:2–3 tells us: "Keep my teaching as the apple of your eye . . . write them on the tablet of your heart." God wants you to know His Word deep in your heart so that you will always remember, and never forget, His love for you and the wonderful plans He has for you! I want to encourage you to speak God's Word out loud each day, just like you wash your face, brush your teeth, and fix your hair.

You can keep this book under your pillow and read it at night or in the morning when you wake up. You can put it in your backpack and share it with friends at school. You can even set aside a special time to read it with your mom, dad, or any of the special people in your life!

The more you speak God's Word out loud, the more you will know what's right from wrong, what's true and false, and what this journey called life is all about. Little by little, you'll become stronger, braver, kinder, and more loving because you'll have His Word working inside of you!

I pray that this book will help you know and understand how loved and treasured you are by God. He loves you more than anything, and He wants you to know about the special purpose you have in His family and the wonderful adventures He has planned for your life!

Love you,
Joyce Meyer

Speaking God's Word About...

Anxiety

Give all your worries and cares to God, for he cares about you.

I PETER 5:7 NLT

Do you ever feel anxious? It's that feeling you get when you're worried about something, like how you'll do on that test at school or whether a friend is mad at you. Maybe you're worried about your mom or dad because they seem sad. Whenever you feel anxious, God is with you and He wants to help you. He cares about everything that you care about, so talk to Him about what's bothering you. You will be okay because God loves you and He's always with you!

We all feel anxious sometimes. Even Jesus! Before His crucifixion, He was in a garden called Gethsemane. He was so anxious, He was sweating blood! He asked God if He really had to go to the cross. Even though He was anxious about His crucifixion, He knew God was with Him. When you're feeling anxious, call on God. He will comfort you!

The Bible says a lot about feeling anxious. Check it out!

"Be strong and courageous. Do not be afraid or terrified because of them, for the Lord your God goes with you; he will never leave you."

DEUTERONOMY 31:6 NIV

I am brave because God is always with me. He will never leave me alone..

I will call to you whenever I'm in trouble, and you will answer me.

PSALM 86:7 NLT

I know God hears me when I tell Him about my worries.

For God has not given us a spirit of fear and timidity, but of power, love, and self-discipline.

2 TIMOTHY 1:7 NLT

God gives me the strength and courage to do what's right when I feel anxious or upset.

He will cover you with his feathers. He will shelter you with his wings. His faithful promises are your armor and protection.

PSALM 91:4 NLT

God always defends and protects me, and I know He will keep me safe.

Don't worry about anything; instead, pray about everything. Tell God what you need, and thank him for all he has done.

PHILIPPIANS 4:6 NLT

I will talk to God about my worries, and I will thank Him for all He has done for me.

Being Kind

Therefore encourage one another and build one another up, just as you are doing.

—I THESSALONIANS 5:11

Kindness is a way of treating people that makes them feel special and loved. It's the way you want to be treated yourself. You can share kindness with anyone, and there are so many ways to do it! You can tell your friend something nice, share your toys with your brother, let someone go first when it's your turn, or help your mom clean up a mess. Kindness is a gift from God, and He wants us to share His gifts with everyone.

My Prayer Today

God, I know that kindness is a fruit of the spirit. Please help me to be kind to everyone I meet today. Amen.

And the Lord's servant must not be quarrelsome but kind to everyone.

2 TIMOTHY 2:24

Because I serve God, I don't argue with people. I am kind to everyone.

Check out what the Bible says about kindness!

Let all that you do be done in love.

—I CORINTHIANS 16:14

I do everything with love.

Kind words are like honey— sweet to the soul and healthy for the body.

—PROVERBS 16:24 NLT

I say nice things to others, and it makes them feel great.

Whoever pursues righteousness and kindness will find life, righteousness, and honor.

—PROVERBS 21:21

When I am good and truthful and kind, I have joy and peace and know I've done a great job.

But the fruit of the Spirit is love, joy, peace, patience, kindness, goodness, faithfulness, gentleness, self-control; against such things there is no law.

—GALATIANS 5:22-23

God has given me everything I need to be like Him—things like His love, joy, peace, patience, kindness, goodness, faithfulness, gentleness, and self-control.

Do to others as you would have them do to you.

—LUKE 6:31 NIV

I treat others the way I want to be treated.

Doing the Right Thing

**And let us not grow weary of doing good,
for in due season we will reap, if we do not give up.**
—GALATIANS 6:9

God lets us make our own choices and we have plenty to make. Sometimes they are small decisions: *Should I spend my money on candy or save up for something better?* Other times they are big decisions: *Should I lie about doing my homework or should I tell the truth?* Our decisions matter more than you know! When you're not sure what to do, ask God to help you think them through.

Let's Talk to God

God, thank You for allowing me
to make my own choices. I pray that
all of my decisions honor You
and make You happy. Amen.

Blessed is the man who fears the Lord, who greatly delights in his commandments!

—PSALM 112:1

God always knows what to do, and I happily do what He says.

He guides me along right paths, bringing honor to his name.

—PSALM 23:3 NLT

God looks out for me and leads me to do what's right.

The Lord will withhold no good thing from those who do what is right.

PSALM 84:11 NLT

If I keep on doing what's right, God will keep on showing me His goodness. He won't hold back!

The fear of the Lord is the beginning of wisdom.

—PROVERBS 9:10

The smartest thing I can do is listen to what God says.

Search me, O God, and know my heart! Try me and know my thoughts! And see if there be any grievous way in me, and lead me in the way everlasting!

—PSALM 139:23–24

God knows what's in my heart and what I'm thinking about. If I'm making the wrong choice, He will show me so I can do the right thing.

Fear

When I am afraid, I put my trust in you.

—PSALM 56:3 NIV

We all feel afraid sometimes. Even Jesus felt afraid. But when Jesus lives inside of you, you don't have to be scared, because He is always with you. Maybe you're feeling afraid because you are going to a new school or you don't like being alone in the dark. Maybe it's because your mom or dad have gone out for the night. Any time you start to feel afraid, all you have to do is ask Jesus to be with you, and He can take that fear away!

Hi! I'm Daniel. I love praying to God and putting my trust in Him. When I had to spend a night in a lions' den because the king didn't want people praying to God, it was scary. But I knew God would protect me, and He did! You can give all your fears to God. He will always be with you.

I prayed to the Lord
and he answered me.
He freed me from
all my fears.

—PSALM 34:4 NLT

*God hears my prayers, and He
takes away all my fears.*

The Bible has a lot to say about fear. Check it out!

Be strong, and let
your heart take
courage, all you who
wait for the Lord!

PSALM 31:24

*God is with me and He helps me.
I'm sure of it!*

"Don't be afraid for I am with
you. Don't be discouraged,
for I am your God. I will
strengthen you and help
you. I will hold you up with
my victorious right hand."

—ISAIAH 41:10 NLT

*I do not have to be afraid because
God is with me. He is on my side,
and He makes me strong.*

The Lord is my light and
my salvation: whom
shall I fear? The Lord
is the stronghold of
my life; of whom
shall I be afraid?

—PSALM 27:1

*God brings light to dark places
and helps me to not be afraid.*

"This is my command—
be strong and courageous!
Do not be afraid or
discouraged. For the
Lord your God is with
you wherever you go."

—JOSHUA 1:9 NLT

*I am strong and brave because
God is always with me.*

Feeling Sad

**The Lord is near to the brokenhearted
and saves the crushed in spirit.**

—PSALM 34:18

We all feel sad sometimes, but God is really good at making us feel better. He cares for us, and He loves to see us laugh and smile! So, when you fall down and get hurt, or when you feel like no one listens to you or understands, or when your heart feels broken, you can run to God and talk to Him about it. He'll fix you right up! God is your best friend, and you can tell Him anything.

Did You Know?

Even Jesus cried sometimes! When He heard that His good friend and follower Lazarus had died, He was very sad, and the Bible says, "Jesus wept." Jesus knows what it's like to feel sad, so the next time you feel sad, turn to Jesus. He can help you feel better.

Check out what the Bible has to say about feeling sad!

You keep track of all my sorrows. You have collected all my tears in your bottle. You have recorded each one in your book.

—PSALM 56:8 NLT

God knows when I'm sad and when I've been crying. He knows what I'm going through, and He will take care of me.

Jesus wept.

—JOHN 11:35

*Jesus cried too.
He knows how I feel.*

Those who look to him are radiant, and their faces shall never be ashamed.

—PSALM 34:5

Thinking about God fills my heart with joy, and my face shows it!

"As a mother comforts her child, so will I comfort you."

—ISAIAH 66:13 NIV

Just like moms comfort their babies, God holds me in His arms until I'm better.

Trust in him at all times, you people; pour out your hearts to him, for God is our refuge.

—PSALM 62:8 NIV

I can always trust God with my true feelings, so I tell Him everything! He is my safe place.

Following God

Jesus said to him, "I am the way, and the truth, and the life. No one comes to the Father except through me."

—JOHN 14:6

The Bible tells us all about God's love for us and all the cool things He wants to help us do. From the very beginning of the Bible, we learn that God made us, and He wants to be a big part of our lives. He knows we won't do everything perfectly. You see, God didn't make us robots. But He wants us to choose for ourselves whether or not we will love Him in return and follow His Word.

Did You Know?

The Apostle Peter was a fisherman. When Jesus asked Peter to be one of His students and to follow Him, Peter didn't hesitate! The Bible says Peter dropped the fishing nets he was holding and followed Jesus right away. What an amazing act of faith!

He guides me along right paths, bringing honor to his name.

—PSALM 23:3 NLT

God gives me good directions.

You have charged us to keep your commandments carefully.

—PSALM 119:4 NLT

I am careful to do what God asks.

I will keep on obeying your instructions forever and ever. I will walk in freedom, for I have devoted myself to your commandments.

—PSALM 119:44–45 NLT

I will always obey what I learn from the Bible, and it will help me to be happy because I'm doing what's right.

See what the Bible says about following God!

Do not merely listen to the word. . . . Do what it says.

—JAMES 1:22 NIV

I don't just listen to God's Word, I do what it says.

Your word is a lamp to my feet and a light to my path.

—PSALM 119:105

God's Word leads me. It keeps me from stumbling around in the dark.

That this is God, our God forever and ever. He will guide us forever.

PSALM 48:14

God is always with me, and I will follow Him and listen to Him forever!

Forgiving

**The Lord our God is merciful and forgiving,
even though we have rebelled against him.**

DANIEL 9:9 NIV

Everybody makes mistakes. And we all need to say, "I'm sorry" sometimes. God says that when we hurt someone else's feelings, we're really hurting Him. But God is always quick to forgive us when we apologize, and He wants us to forgive ourselves quickly too—and then try to do the right thing next time. God also asks us to do the same thing and forgive other people when they hurt our feelings. He teaches us to love people perfectly, just like He does.

Hi! I'm known as the Prodigal Son. I once ran away from home, and when I decided to return, I was worried my father would be angry. But as soon as he saw me, he forgave me! God also forgives us when we do things we're not supposed to. God wants you to forgive too, even when it's hard! Ask Him to help you forgive others.

The Bible says a lot about forgiveness. Check it out!

For all have sinned and fall short of the glory of God, and are justified by his grace.

ROMANS 3:23–24

God always forgives me when I ask Him to and shows me the right thing to do.

Your sins are forgiven for his name's sake.

—I JOHN 2:12

I am forgiven because of what Jesus did for me.

"For if you forgive other people when they sin against you, your heavenly Father will also forgive you."

MATTHEW 6:14 NIV

God wants me to forgive other people, just like He forgives me.

Love prospers when a fault is forgiven, but dwelling on it separates close friends.

PROVERBS 17:9 NLT

I become closer to my friends and family when I forgive them for things that have hurt me.

As the Lord has forgiven you, so you also must forgive.

—COLOSSIANS 3:13

Just like God forgives me, when someone hurts me, I need to forgive them.

"So if the Son sets you free, you will be free indeed."

—JOHN 8:36

God forgives me so I can forget my mistakes and love my life every day!

God Always Comes Through

Behold, the eye of the Lord is on those who fear him, on those who hope in his steadfast love.

—PSALM 33:18

Have you ever wondered: *Is God listening to my prayers?* Or, *When is He ever going to come help me?* Lots of us can feel that way when we're waiting to see the answers to our prayers. Sometimes we have to wait a long, long time, but God *always* hears us and has a good reason for the wait. He knows what's best for us! And what He wants you to know down deep in your heart is that if you put your hope in Him, He will always come through. And when He does, you'll have so much fun telling your friends about the amazing things God did for you.

My Prayer Today

God, thank You for doing what's best for me, even when my prayers aren't answered right away. Amen.

Check out what the Bible says about God's faithfulness!

"The Lord is my portion," says my soul, "therefore I will hope in him."

—LAMENTATIONS 3:24

God gives me everything I need. He never lets me down.

Rejoice in hope, be patient in tribulation, be constant in prayer.

—ROMANS 12:12

Hope makes me happy! I am peaceful even when life is hard, and I have to be patient. I pray all the time.

"In this world you will have trouble. But take heart! I have overcome the world."

—JOHN 16:33 NIV

When I have a problem, I talk to God about it. He makes everything better because He is a big God!

Jesus Christ is the same yesterday, today, and forever.

—HEBREWS 13:8

Jesus is always, always, always the same!

Having hope will give you courage. You will be protected and will rest in safety. You will lie down unafraid, and many will look to you for help.

—JOB 11:18-19 NLT

Hope gives me courage, and God protects me. I don't have to be afraid, and I can help others be unafraid too!

God Is a Big God!

"Look! The Lamb of God who
takes away the sin of the world!"

—JOHN 1:29 NLT

No one can say how big and strong and powerful God is, but it sure is fun to think about! The Bible says He made the whole world in six days! He placed the sun, moon, and stars in the sky. He parted the waters of the Red Sea so His people could go free. He can move a mountain if you really need Him to. God is so strong and powerful that nothing on earth or in heaven can ever stand against Him.

I'm Moses, and with God's help, I led the Israelites out of Egypt. When we were on the run from Pharaoh's army, God split the Red Sea so there was a path of dry land for us to walk on. We crossed the sea and escaped Pharaoh without ever getting wet! God is bigger and more powerful than you can imagine!

With a mighty hand and outstretched arm; His love endures forever.

—PSALM 136:12 NIV

God's love for me never runs out. It goes on forever!

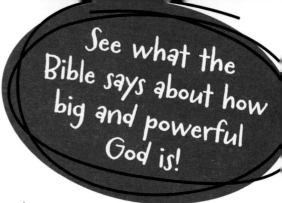

See what the Bible says about how big and powerful God is!

God saw all that he had made, and it was very good. . . . Thus the heavens and the earth were completed in all their vast array.

—GENESIS 1:31; 2:1 NIV

Everything God makes is good! From all the birds to the plants and animals that live on the earth and in the sea . . . and even me!

"Yours, O Lord, is the greatness and the power and the glory and the victory and the majesty, for all that is in the heavens and in the earth is yours."

—I CHRONICLES 29:11

God made everything, and it all belongs to Him.

He will not grow tired or weary, and his understanding no one can fathom.

ISAIAH 40:28 NIV

God never gets tired. He never has to go to sleep. And no one is as smart as He is.

I am the Lord, and there is no other. I form light and create darkness; I make well-being and create calamity; I am the Lord, who does all these things.

—ISAIAH 45:6–7

God is the only God. He made daytime and nighttime. He knows what He's doing.

29

God Is Good!

The steadfast love of the Lord never ceases; his mercies never come to an end; they are new every morning; great is your faithfulness.

—LAMENTATIONS 3:22-23

If there's one thing you should know about God, it's that He is good. The Bible tells us that God loves us more than anything—and that will never change. That means no matter what you do (or don't do), His love for you will always be the same. Plus, God wants you to enjoy each day of your life, and He has lots of fun adventures planned for you. All you have to do is what His Word tells you to do.

My Prayer Today

God, I know that You are good. Thank You for always loving me and taking care of me. Teach me how to love You with my whole heart! Amen.

Check out what the Bible says about God's goodness!

Taste and see that the Lord is good; blessed is the one who takes refuge in him.

—PSALM 34:8 NIV

God is good! I can run to Him for help.

And may you have the power to understand, as all God's people should, how wide, how long, how high, and how deep his love is.

—EPHESIANS 3:18 NLT

God wants me to understand just how huge His love is for me.

The steadfast love of the Lord never ceases; his mercies never come to an end.

LAMENTATIONS 3:22

God's love never ends, and He always forgives.

Give thanks to the Lord, for he is good. His love endures forever.

—PSALM 136:1 NIV

I thank God! He is good, and His love goes on forever.

The Lord is good to all; he has compassion on all he has made.

—PSALM 145:9 NIV

God is good! He cares for me and everything He's made.

Every good gift and perfect gift is from above.

—JAMES 1:17

Everything that's good comes from God.

God Keeps Me Safe

If God is for us, who can be against us?

—ROMANS 8:31

God is our Dad, and He is always with us. He watches over us very carefully to keep us safe from harm. Just like we wear helmets when we ride our bikes and learn to look both ways before we cross the street, God tells us in His Word the things we can do to avoid accidents and keep ourselves from getting hurt. When people are mean to you or you don't feel safe, God wants you to call out to Him for help. He will always come running to help you.

Hi! We're Shadrach, Meshach, and Abednego. We love to worship God, but the king wanted the people to worship him. When he found out we were still praying to God, the king was very angry! He heated up a fire and threw us inside! But God appeared in the fire with us, and we stepped out unharmed. God always protects us!

Even when I walk through the darkest valley, I will not be afraid, for you are close beside me. Your rod and your staff protect and comfort me.

—PSALM 23:4 NLT

Even when scary things happen, I don't have to be afraid because God is with me. He comforts me and keeps me safe.

The Bible says a lot about God's protection. Check it out!

"Though the mountains be shaken and the hills be removed, yet my unfailing love for you will not be shaken nor my covenant of peace be removed," says the Lord, who has compassion on you.

—ISAIAH 54:10 NIV

When crazy or scary things happen, God's love and His promises remain the same. He's got me and He cares for me.

He will cover you with his feathers. He will shelter you with his wings. His faithful promises are your armor and protection. Do not be afraid of the terrors of the night, nor the arrow that flies in the day.

—PSALM 91:4–5 NLT

God guards me and keeps me safe, like a mama bird guards her nest. I don't have to be scared during the day or when I go to sleep at night.

The name of the Lord is a strong tower; the righteous man runs into it and is safe.

—PROVERBS 18:10

Jesus' name is powerful! I call His name and He keeps me safe.

33

Help Me!

**My help comes from the Lord,
who made heaven and earth.**

—PSALM 121:2

When you're having a hard time with something, it's really smart to ask for help. It could be that you need help learning a new skill like tying your shoes or casting a fishing rod. Or maybe the zipper on your backpack got stuck. Sometimes we have much bigger problems than that, but God gave us friends and family to help us. And He will help us too! All we have to do is ask.

Let's Talk to God

God, please help me to remember that I can always lean on You, and You will give me what I need! Thank You.

God is our refuge and strength, a very present help in trouble.

—PSALM 46:1

God keeps me safe and strong. If I have trouble with anything, He's right there to help me.

Trust in the Lord with all your heart, and do not lean on your own understanding.

—PROVERBS 3:5

I trust God with all my heart. I don't try to do things my own way.

When the righteous call for help, the Lord hears and delivers them out of all their troubles.

—PSALM 34:17

I'm God's kid. So when I need help, He hears me and comes to rescue me.

Let us then with confidence draw near to the throne of grace, that we may receive mercy and find grace to help in time of need.

—HEBREWS 4:16

I run to God for help. He is kind and forgiving, and He always helps me out.

Jesus looked at them and said, "With man this is impossible, but with God all things are possible."

—MATTHEW 19:26 NIV

Some things are too hard for me, but nothing is too hard for God.

How I Feel

**Above all else, guard your heart,
for everything you do flows from it.**
—PROVERBS 4:23 NIV

Feelings are funny things. We can be giggly and silly one minute and then sad or mad the next. But no matter what we are feeling, we can be open and honest about it with God. He wants us to know that He understands how we feel, and we don't have to pretend that we are just fine when we really feel bad on the inside. God also wants us to know that we can go to His Word to be comforted and encouraged. He loves to build us up!

My Prayer Today

Lord, thank You for listening to my concerns.
Help me to turn to Your Word when
I'm feeling sad or discouraged, and
remind me to thank You when
I'm feeling happy or grateful. Amen.

The Bible says a lot about our feelings. Check it out!

Rejoice with those who rejoice, weep with those who weep.

—ROMANS 12:15

When someone is happy, I'm happy for them! When someone is sad, I'm sad with them.

Give all your worries and cares to God, for he cares about you.

—1 PETER 5:7 NLT

I can give my worries to God because He cares about me.

Why am I discouraged? Why is my heart so sad? I will put my hope in God! I will praise Him again— my Savior and my God!

—PSALM 42:5-6 NLT

I don't have to be sad or discouraged, because I have hope in God. He is awesome!

You have turned my mourning into joyful dancing.

—PSALM 30:11 NLT

God took away my sadness. Now I'm doing a happy dance!

A joyful heart is good medicine, but a crushed spirit dries up the bones.

PROVERBS 17:22

A happy heart makes me feel better. But being in a bad mood takes all my energy away.

Restore to me the joy of your salvation, and make me willing to obey you.

PSALM 51:12 NLT

When I lose my joy, God can help me get it back!

37

Hurt Feelings

No weapon that is fashioned against you shall succeed.

—ISAIAH 54:17

Has someone ever made you feel bad about being you? Maybe they picked on you or didn't include you in a party or a game. Maybe they took something away from you, pushed or hit you, or something even worse. Well, no matter what people say or do to you, God thinks you're special and He loves you just the way you are. He cares about everything that happens to you—and He wants to help you when you're hurting. Here's what God says you should think, say, and do when someone bullies you.

My Prayer Today

God, sometimes people hurt my feelings and make me feel bad. Help me to remember that no matter what, You will always love me and take care of me. Amen.

And we know that in all things God works for the good of those who love him, who have been called according to his purpose.

—ROMANS 8:28 NIV

Everything will work out for my good! God says so.

Check out what the Bible says about God's care for you!

If God is for us, who can be against us?

—ROMANS 8:31

It doesn't matter if someone doesn't like me, because God is on my side.

Weeping may stay for the night, but rejoicing comes in the morning.

—PSALM 30:5 NIV

Even though things are really hard right now, God is always with me. And things will get better!

"Be strong and courageous. Do not fear or be in dread of them, for it is the Lord your God who goes with you. He will not leave you or forsake you."

—DEUTERONOMY 31:6

I am strong and brave. Even when someone is mean to me, I'm not afraid because God is with me. He's not going anywhere.

See what kind of love the Father has given to us, that we should be called children of God; and so we are. The reason why the world does not know us is that it did not know him.

—I JOHN 3:1

God loves me and calls me His child—and that's who I am. Those who mistreat me don't know what they're doing, because they don't know God.

I Can Do It!

**Never be lazy, but work hard
and serve the Lord enthusiastically.**

—ROMANS 12:11 NLT

Sometimes we're given a job that's tough, like when your mom asks you to pick up your toys or clean your room and you just don't feel like helping. But God knows what you are capable of—and you can come to Him for help. When you are tired or frustrated and feel like giving up, ask God to help you change your attitude. If you keep on keeping on with a good attitude, you will be surprised what you can do with God's help.

My name is David. I was a boy when God called me to fight a giant named Goliath. Everyone thought I was too small to beat him. But God strengthened me with His Spirit, and I defeated Goliath with just a slingshot and a stone! You can do things you may think are too hard because God gives you strength.

I can do all things through him who strengthens me.

—PHILIPPIANS 4:13

I can do everything I need to do with God's help!

He who is in you is greater than he who is in the world.

—I JOHN 4:4

God lives in me— and He's stronger than anything.

Whatever your hand finds to do, do it with all your might.

—ECCLESIASTES 9:10 NIV

Whatever job I have to do, I will do it well. I give God my very best.

God is our refuge and strength, a very present help in trouble.

PSALM 46:1

With God by my side, I can do anything.

No, in all these things we are more than conquerors through him who loved us.

—ROMANS 8:37 NIV

I can tackle anything I need to do because God helps me.

But they who wait for the Lord shall renew their strength; they shall mount up with wings like eagles.

—ISAIAH 40:31

When I get tired, I trust God to give me new strength. He gives me so much that I feel like I can do anything.

I Choose to Be Happy

**All the days of the afflicted are evil,
but the cheerful of heart has a continual feast.**

—PROVERBS 15:15

Have you ever had a day when things just didn't go your way? Maybe your friend got picked for the baseball team and you didn't. Maybe your brother took the last piece of pizza when you were hoping for another slice. Or you wished you had cool clothes or a bike like another kid down the street. God wants you to know that He understands—and He wants to help you have a great day anyway!

Did You Know?

It makes God happy when you're happy. Smiling when you're in a grumpy mood can make you feel happier. Try it! The next time you're feeling down, look in the mirror and give yourself a big smile and thank God for all the good things He's given you. Don't you feel better?

See what the Bible says about choosing to be happy!

Give thanks in all circumstances; for this is the will of God in Christ Jesus for you.

—I THESSALONIANS 5:18

I'm glad when things work out for me, and I'm even thankful when they don't. God wants me to be happy either way!

Do everything without grumbling or arguing.

—PHILIPPIANS 2:14 NIV

I do whatever I have to do without arguing or complaining.

I will give to the Lord and the thanks due to his righteousness, and I will sing praise to the name of the Lord, the Most High.

—PSALM 7:17

I will tell the Lord how good He is. I will sing songs to Him. And praise Him.

Let us come into his presence with thanksgiving; let us make a joyful noise to him with songs of praise! For the Lord is a great God, and a great King above all gods.

—PSALM 95:2–3

I come to God with a happy heart and celebrate Him by singing because no one is like Him. He's the greatest.

Be content with what you have, because God has said, "Never will I leave you; never will I forsake you."

—HEBREWS 13:5 NIV

God is always with me, and that's all I need to be happy.

I Love God!

**Glorify the Lord with me;
let us exalt his name together.**
—PSALM 34:3 NIV

God is easy to love. He is always here with us—and He has already done so much for us. Sometimes we forget just how good God is. When that happens, it helps to start thinking about the things He's done for us in the past—and to find special ways to say thank You. You can sing Him a song, make some creative artwork, or best of all . . . you can share His love with someone else!

Let's Talk to God

God, I love You so much!
Help me to show You my love
today and every day. Amen.

We know and rely on the love God has for us. God is love. Whoever lives in love lives in God, and God in them.

—1 JOHN 4:16 NIV

I know God loves me. God is love. Because He gives me His love, I have plenty to share with others.

The Bible says a lot about loving God. Check it out!

Come, let us worship and bow down. Let us kneel before the Lord our maker, for he is our God.

—PSALM 95:6–7 NLT

I sing and shout about how good God is! And I serve Him because He made me.

Has the Lord redeemed you? Then speak out! Tell others he has redeemed you from your enemies.

—PSALM 107:2 NLT

God loves me, and He gave me a brand-new life! I want everyone to know how good He is.

Bless the Lord, O my soul, and forget not all his benefits.

—PSALM 103:2

I love God! I'll never forget the good things He's done for me.

Loving God means keeping his commandments, and his commandments are not burdensome.

—1 JOHN 5:3 NLT

I love God and I love His Word. So it's not too hard to do what's right.

I'm in God's Family

**See how very much our Father loves us,
for he calls us his children, and that is what we are!**

—I JOHN 3:1 NLT

God chose you to be in His family—and that is so cool! God's family is the best family ever because it's full of all kinds of different people from all over the world. One day we'll all be in heaven together, celebrating all the wonderful things God has done. But we don't have to wait until then to get to know one another. We can help and pray for each other right here, right now!

Did You Know?

Joseph had eleven brothers. That's a pretty big family! Maybe you think your family is only your mom and dad and sister, or maybe you don't feel like you have any family at all. But you are part of God's family, and that means you're related to people all over the world through God. Isn't that amazing?

"I will be a Father to you, and you will be my sons and daughters, says the Lord Almighty."

—2 CORINTHIANS 6:18 NIV

God is my Dad, and I am His child.

Even before he made the world, God loved us and chose us in Christ to be holy and without fault in his eyes.

—EPHESIANS 1:4 NLT

Even before God made the world, He loved me and picked me to be like Him.

There is neither Jew nor Greek, there is neither slave nor free, there is no male and female, for you are all one in Christ Jesus.

—GALATIANS 3:28

God's family is made up of all kinds of different people— but He loves us all the same. We are family!

God decided in advance to adopt us into his own family by bringing us to himself through Jesus Christ. This is what he wanted to do, and it gave him great pleasure.

—EPHESIANS 1:5 NLT

Because of Jesus, I'm part of God's family.

Once you were not a people, but now you are God's people; once you had not received mercy, but now you have received mercy.

—I PETER 2:10

I am part of God's family, and He loves me and calls me His kid.

It's a Good Day!

These things I have spoken to you, that my joy may be in you, and that your joy may be full.

Every day is a gift from God—and He wants us to enjoy every minute! Some days are better than others, but no matter what's going on, we can always find our joy in Jesus. When nothing seems to be going right, remember that God is still God and He is always here for you. Ask Him for some help and encouragement, and then trust Him to give it to you. You can start to turn a bad day upside down by reading about how much God loves you in His Word!

Let's Talk to God

God, thank You for the gift of today!
Let everything I do today
glorify and honor You. Amen

"And do not be grieved, for the joy of the Lord is your strength."

—NEHEMIAH 8:10

I don't have to be sad. God gave me His joy to make me strong.

"The thief comes only to steal and kill and destroy. I came that they may have life and have it abundantly."

—JOHN 10:10

While the devil wants to give me bad days, Jesus came to save me and give me an amazing life with Him!

For you, O Lord, have made me glad by your work; at the works of your hands I sing for joy.

PSALM 92:4

Seeing everything God created makes me so happy I could sing!

This is the day that the Lord has made; let us rejoice and be glad in it.

—PSALM 118:24

God made this day and I'm going to enjoy it and be happy.

Let everything that has breath praise the Lord! Praise the Lord!

—PSALM 150:6

As long as I live, I'll be thankful to God.

Rejoice in the Lord always; again I will say, rejoice.

—PHILIPPIANS 4:4

I'm happy because of what God has done for me. I'll say it again: I'm happy!

Just Say No!

So humble yourselves before God.
Resist the devil, and he will flee from you.

—JAMES 4:7 NLT

Have you ever been tempted to do something that you know you shouldn't do? Maybe you gobbled down three cookies when your mom said you could have only two. Or you went to play with friends instead of cleaning up your room. God gives us the freedom to choose what we will do. But He wants us to know that wrong choices bring wrong results, and right choices bring right results. The good news is, with God's help, we can always say no to temptation.

My Prayer Today

God, I want to do what is right.
Help me to resist temptation
and make good choices. Thank You.

For because he himself has suffered when tempted, he is able to help those who are being tempted.

—HEBREWS 2:18

It's hard to say no to temptation, but Jesus knows how I feel and He's here to help me.

"Keep watch and pray, so that you will not give in to temptation."

—MARK 14:38 NLT

The devil is sneaky, but I know God's voice and I am careful to listen to Him and pray.

I have stored up your word in my heart, that I might not sin against you.

—PSALM 119:11

Little by little, I'm learning God's Word so that I can do what it says.

[Jesus] understands our weaknesses, for he faced all of the same testings we do.

—HEBREWS 4:15 NLT

Sometimes I feel weak, and Jesus gets that. But He kept going, and I want to be like Him!

God blesses those who patiently endure testing and temptation. Afterward they will receive the crown of life that God has promised to those who love him.

—JAMES 1:12 NLT

I do what God asks without complaining and He takes good care of me.

Loving My Family and Friends

Let all that you do be done in love.

—I CORINTHIANS 16:14

God wants us to be kind and show love to our family and friends. But sometimes getting along with people is hard work. There will be times when you aren't getting along at all, and you don't really want to be loving and patient and kind. But if you ask God to show you how to love your family and friends, you can trust Him to help you. He is always here for you!

My Prayer Today

Jesus, thank You for all the wonderful family and friends You've given me. Please help me to treat them with kindness and love, even when it's hard! Amen.

Live in harmony with one another.

—ROMANS 12:16

I do my best to get along with others.

The Bible says a lot about loving others. Check it out!

Submit to one another out of reverence for Christ.

—EPHESIANS 5:21 NIV

I put others first because Jesus asks me to.

"A new commandment I give to you, that you love one another; just as I have loved you, you also are to love one another."

—JOHN 13:34

I follow Jesus' example to love others the way He has loved me.

"Greater love has no one than this, that someone lay down his life for his friends."

—JOHN 15:13

There's no greater way I can show love than to put my friends and family first.

We love because he first loved us.

1 JOHN 4:19

I can love others because God loved us first. He taught me how.

Children, obey your parents in the Lord, for this is right. "Honor your father and mother" (this is the first commandment with a promise).

—EPHESIANS 6:1–2

I do what my parents tell me and treat them with respect because God asked me to.

Obeying

Do not merely listen to the word. . . . Do what it says.

—JAMES 1:22 NIV

Do you remember what that sneaky old serpent said to Eve in the Garden of Eden? (See Genesis 3:1.) He said, "Did God really say you shouldn't eat from this tree? Its fruit looks so good." He made disobeying God seem like a good thing. He wanted Adam and Eve to break God's rules. That's because Satan hates God, and he didn't want Adam and Eve to be friends with God. Well, Satan doesn't want us to be friends with God either. But the truth is, God loves us and if we do what He says, or what our parents and those who love us say, He promises to take care of us.

I'm Noah. God spoke to me and told me to build an ark for my family and all the animals, because He was going to cover the earth in a flood. Everyone thought I was crazy! But I trusted God, and He saved me and my family! If you hear God telling you to do something, obey Him. He wants what is best for you!

"The Lord our God we will serve, and his voice we will obey."

—JOSHUA 24:24

I listen for God's voice and I do what He says.

The Bible has a lot to say about obedience. Check it out!

Teach me to do your will, for you are my God.

—PSALM 143:10 NIV

God, teach me to follow You and do what You ask.

Children, obey your parents in everything, for this pleases the Lord.

—COLOSSIANS 3:20

I obey my parents because it makes God happy.

"You shall have no other gods before me."

—DEUTERONOMY 5:7 NIV

In my heart, God always comes first.

Jesus replied, "Anyone who loves me will obey my teaching.

JOHN 14:23

I love Jesus and I follow what He says.

For the Lord corrects those he loves, just as a father corrects a child in whom he delights.

—PROVERBS 3:12 NLT

When God shows me that I'm doing something wrong, it's because He loves me—He's my Dad and He's looking out for me.

Patience

Patience is better than pride.

—ECCLESIASTES 7:8 NLT

Even though it may not always feel like it, waiting is good for us! It gives us a chance to think things over and helps us calm down on the inside, so we don't make hurried decisions. Waiting is a normal, everyday part of life. We wait for green lights when we're driving in the car, for the season to change . . . and for our birthday to finally arrive. And while we are waiting, God wants us to be peaceful. He doesn't want us to feel anxious or to get upset with others. He wants us to enjoy every moment—and with His help, we can! Just remember this: things take time, and God is on your side.

My name is Sarah. I always wanted to have a baby, but I was an old woman before God blessed me with one. I had to be very patient and believe that God could do anything. And He did! I finally was blessed with the child I always wanted.

See what the Bible says about being patient!

Whoever is patient has great understanding, but one who is quick-tempered displays folly.

—PROVERBS 14:29 NIV

I am patient with others, and not easily upset.

I wait quietly before God, for my victory comes from him.

—PSALM 62:1 NLT

I never have to yell for God to move faster. I know He's looking out for me.

A hot-tempered person stirs up conflict, but the one who is patient calms a quarrel.

—PROVERBS 15:18 NIV

I am calm and patient, and when my friends get upset, I help calm them down.

Wait for the Lord and keep his way, and he will exalt you to inherit the land.

—PSALM 37:34

While I'm waiting, I keep on doing what God says. I know He'll come through.

We also pray that you will be strengthened with all his glorious power so you will have all the endurance and patience you need.

—COLOSSIANS 1:11 NLT

God gives me the strength I need to be patient.

Peace and Quiet

"I am leaving you with a gift—peace of mind and heart."

—JOHN 14:27 NLT

Did you know that God's peace is amazing? Peace is a calm feeling inside of you that everything is all right. You can have God's peace and stay at rest on the inside because God is with you. And we can also live in peace with one another. God gave you His gift of peace for keeps. So, whether you're playing with your friends or having some quiet time, you can always be at peace. Here's what's really cool: God's peace in you is a sign to others that God lives inside you!

Did You Know?

God loves when you talk to Him, and God also loves to talk to you! The Bible says that God's voice is usually very quiet, like a whisper in your ear. In order to hear Him, you have to get quiet, calm your mind, and listen. Try it the next time you want to feel God's peace within you.

And a harvest of righteousness is sown in peace by those who make peace.

JAMES 3:18

When I do what is right, it makes me feel more peaceful.

And let the peace that comes from Christ rule in your hearts.

—COLOSSIANS 3:15 NLT

The same peace that Jesus has is inside of me!

Strive for peace with everyone, and for the holiness without which no one will see the Lord.

—HEBREWS 12:14

I try to be peaceful with everyone and to love God with all my heart.

You will keep in perfect peace those whose minds are steadfast, because they trust in you.

—ISAIAH 26:3 NIV

I have lots of peace because I keep God in all my thoughts, and I trust Him no matter what.

Seek peace and pursue it.

—I PETER 3:11

Wherever God's peace is, that's where I go.

If it is possible, as far as it depends on you, live at peace with everyone.

—ROMANS 12:18 NIV

Instead of picking fights, I bring peace instead.

Putting God and Others First

It is no longer I who live, but Christ who lives in me. And the life I now live in the flesh I live by faith in the Son of God, who loved me and gave himself for me.

—GALATIANS 2:20

When Jesus was here on earth, He didn't just live for Himself. He lived to serve His Father in heaven and all the people on earth. He taught us by example to love others with a selfless love—the kind that puts others first. He loved us so much that He gave His life to give us life. And we can thank God by putting Him and others first.

Did You Know?

In the Bible, Jesus says the last will be first. Doesn't that sound a little backward? Not with God! This means that those who are humble, live selflessly, and serve others will have a special place in heaven.

He made himself nothing
by taking the very
nature of a servant.

—PHILIPPIANS 2:7 NIV

*Like Jesus, I am
here to help others.*

See what the Bible says about serving God and others!

Serve one another
humbly in love.

—GALATIANS 5:13 NIV

I simply serve others, with love.

"If anyone forces you
to go one mile, go with
them two miles."

MATTHEW 5:41 NIV

*When someone asks me for help,
I do even more for them than what
they've asked me to do.*

The greatest among you
shall be your servant.

—MATTHEW 23:11

*Loving and serving others
is the best choice I can make.*

Love one another
with brotherly
affection. Outdo
one another
in showing honor.

—ROMANS 12:10

*I love others like they're my
own brothers or sisters.
I let them know they're amazing
every chance I get.*

Don't be selfish;
don't try to impress
others. Be humble,
thinking of others
as better than yourselves.

—PHILIPPIANS 2:3 NLT

*I am not selfish or a show-off.
I am more concerned about
others than I am about myself.*

Rejection

"I have loved you with an everlasting love;
therefore I have continued my faithfulness to you."

—JEREMIAH 31:3

It's a terrible feeling when you're picked last to be on someone's team or you aren't invited to a birthday party that "everyone" is going to. No one wants to be left out or forgotten. That's what rejection feels like. One awesome thing about God is He never, ever forgets you or leaves you alone. He always chooses you to be on His "team." So whenever you're sad because someone didn't include you or choose you, remember that God thinks you're wonderful and He loves you!

Did You Know?

Joseph faced rejection from his own family. His brothers were jealous of him and hated him. They sold him as a slave in Eygpt, and then they told their father that Joseph had died. But God was with Joseph through all that rejection and made him one of the most powerful men in Egypt! He is with you in your rejection too.

The Bible has a lot to say about rejection. Check it out!

"I will live among you, and I will not despise you."

—LEVITICUS 26:11 NLT

God is always with me, and no matter what, He will never stop loving me.

"I chose you."

—JOHN 15:16

God loves me and He always picks me.

God has said, "Never will I leave you; never will I forsake you."

—HEBREWS 13:5 NIV

Everywhere I go and whatever I do, I know God is with me and I can do all things with Him.

If God is for us, who can be against us?

—ROMANS 8:31

Because God is always on my side, it doesn't matter what anyone else does or says to hurt me.

"Be strong and courageous. Do not be afraid; do not be discouraged, for the Lord your God will be with you wherever you go."

—JOSHUA 1:9 NIV

God made me strong and courageous! I will always remember that He is with me and He loves and cares for me.

Saying I'm Sorry

Therefore confess your sins to each other and pray for each other so that you may be healed.

JAMES 5:16

We all mess up sometimes and hurt someone's feelings. Maybe you were mad and said something mean to a friend, or you were unkind to your mom or dad when they told you to do something. When you make a mistake like this, the best thing you can do is talk to God and tell Him you're sorry. Ask Him to help you and then go to the person you hurt and tell them you're sorry too. It's not easy to apologize, but afterward, you'll feel so much better.

Let's Talk to God

God, sometimes it's really hard to apologize when I do something wrong. Help me to say sorry when I disobey or hurt someone's feelings. Amen.

There is therefore now no condemnation for those who are in Christ Jesus.

—ROMANS 8:1

After I say, "I'm sorry," I don't have to think about my mistakes anymore because of what Jesus did for me.

The Bible says a lot about apologizing. Check it out!

If we confess our sins, he is faithful and just to forgive us our sins and to cleanse us from all unrighteousness.

I JOHN 1:9

God forgives me when I tell Him about my mistakes.

So then let us pursue what makes for peace and for mutual upbuilding.

ROMANS 14:19

I say, "I'm sorry" when I am wrong and do what I can to make things right with others.

Be kind to one another, tenderhearted, forgiving one another, as God in Christ forgave you.

—EPHESIANS 4:32

I am kind toward others. I am quick to say, "I'm sorry," and forgive others too.

"And whenever you stand praying, forgive, if you have anything against anyone, so that your Father also who is in heaven may forgive you your trespasses."

—MARK 11:25-26

When I'm talking to God, I will ask Him to help me forgive those who hurt me. When I mess up, I will say, "I'm sorry."

Sharing

Whoever gives to the poor will not want.

—PROVERBS 28:27

Sharing with our friends is a good thing. There's always a chance your friend won't share what they have with you, but God wants you to know that you don't ever have to be afraid to share with others. He will always take care of you. And God is more generous than every person put together. The truth is, when you share anything—a hug, a cookie, or a game you're playing with—it makes God happy, and it makes you and your friend feel good on the inside too. Sharing is just another way of saying, "I care about you."

My name is Elijah. Once, God spoke to me and told me to visit a widow and ask her for food. She didn't have much—only a little oil and flour! But she made a loaf of bread and shared it with me, and God made sure her supply of food never ran out! God loves when you share what you have with others.

Each one must give as he has decided in his heart, not reluctantly or under compulsion, for God loves a cheerful giver.

—2 CORINTHIANS 9:7

When I give something away, I give it with a glad heart. God loves a cheerful giver.

Check out what the Bible says about sharing!

"It is more blessed to give than to receive."

—ACTS 20:35

It's better for me to give than to get.

Whatever you give is acceptable if you give it eagerly. And give according to what you have, not what you don't have.

—2 CORINTHIANS 8:12 NLT

I am excited to help others, no matter how much I have to give, whether it's a little or a lot.

"Give, and you will receive. Your gift will return to you in full—pressed down, shaken together to make room for more, running over, and poured into your lap."

—LUKE 6:38 NLT

When I give to others, it makes God happy and He wants to bless me even more!

"Be on your guard against all kinds of greed; life does not consist in an abundance of possessions."

—LUKE 12:15 NIV

There is more to life than having "stuff." So, I am happy to share what I have.

Taking Care of My Stuff

The earth is the Lord's, and everything in it.

—PSALM 24:1 NLT

God wants us to take care of our bodies, our homes, our "stuff," our neighborhoods, our world and each other. One way we can honor God is to take care of all the things He's given us. If we prove to be good caretakers of little things, then God will entrust us with bigger things.

Did You Know?

One day, Jesus was visiting a woman named Mary. She had some very expensive perfume and poured it on Jesus' head. Mary's friends were upset because they thought she had wasted the perfume! But Jesus was pleased that she had sacrificed something so precious. God loves when we use the things we have to bless others.

Lazy hands make for poverty, but diligent hands bring wealth.

—PROVERBS 10:4 NIV

Being lazy won't help me at all, but working hard brings rewards.

Every good and every perfect gift is from above, coming down from the Father of lights, with whom there is no variation or shadow due to change.

—JAMES 1:17

Every gift I have comes from God, who doesn't change. He is always the same.

"Wealth and honor come from you alone, for you rule over everything."

—1 CHRONICLES 29:12 NLT

All my gifts, talents, and the things I own come from God. He is in charge of everything.

"One who is faithful in a very little is also faithful in much."

—LUKE 16:10

When I take good care of what God has given me, He can trust me to take care of more.

"And if you have not been faithful in that which is another's, who will give you that which is your own?"

—LUKE 16:12

If I take good care of other people's things, then I can be trusted to have my own things to take care of.

69

Talking to God

**The Lord is near to all who call on him,
to all who call on him in truth.**

—PSALM 145:18

Did you know that you can talk to God about anything? Sometimes He'll answer with a really peaceful feeling. Or He'll speak to you in what the Bible calls a "gentle whisper" or a "still, small voice" (see 1 Kings 19:12). God talks to you when you read the Bible and also through the Holy Spirit. He comforts you, helps you figure things out, and stands by to lend you a hand. God is always listening, and He can't wait to hear from you!

Hi! My name is Samuel. I was asleep in my bed one night and I heard someone call my name. I thought it was my teacher Eli, but it was God! I answered, "Here I am!" God can speak to anyone, even little ones! When you feel nervous, excited, joyful, or angry, talk to God about it. He listens, and He answers.

"Ask, and it will be given to you; seek, and you will find; knock, and it will be opened to you."

MATTHEW 7:7

I ask God for help and He helps me. I look for Him and He's there. When I knock on God's door, He always answers.

The Bible says a lot about talking to God. Check it out!

So let us come boldly to the throne of our gracious God. There we will receive his mercy, and we will find grace to help us when we need it most.

—HEBREWS 4:16 NLT

I pray to God right away. I know He will forgive me for my sins and help me when I need it most.

"Ask and you will receive, and your joy will be complete."

—JOHN 16:24 NIV

I ask God for what I need, and I am full of joy because I know He will help me.

And this is the confidence that we have toward him, that if we ask anything according to his will he hears us.

—I JOHN 5:14

I trust God to answer my prayers in the way that's best for me, and He does.

I love the Lord, because he has heard my voice and my pleas for mercy. Because he inclined his ear to me, therefore I will call on him as long as I live.

—PSALM 116:1–2

I love God because He leans close and hears my voice. I could talk to Him forever.

Telling the Truth

**So I strive always to keep my conscience
clear before God and man.**

—ACTS 24:16 NIV

Have you ever lied to your parents, broken something by accident, or done something you know was wrong—and you wished you could make it better? Well, sometimes accidents happen, and sometimes we even do the wrong thing on purpose. When you mess up, the best thing to do is tell the truth to God and your parents or whoever you need to tell the truth to. God still loves us, and He is always willing to forgive us, no matter what we've done. And the good news is, after we've told the truth, God gives us back His peace and joy . . . and we feel a lot better on the inside.

My Prayer Today

God, please help me to tell the truth, even when it's not easy. Thank You for always forgiving me when I do things I'm not supposed to. I love You!

The Bible has a lot to say about honesty. Check it out!

I am speaking the truth in Christ—I am not lying; my conscience bears me witness in the Holy Spirt.

—ROMANS 9:1

I tell the truth, and the Holy Spirit gives me confidence.

"So set yourselves apart to be holy, for I am the Lord your God."

—LEVITICUS 20:7 NLT

I belong to God, so I do what is right.

If you want to enjoy life and see many happy days, keep your tongue from speaking evil and your lips from telling lies.

—I PETER 3:10–12 NLT

I want to have a good, long life. So, I think before I speak, and I don't tell lies.

A dishonest man spreads strife, and a whisperer separates close friends.

—PROVERBS 16:28

I don't stir up trouble or whisper lies that ruin my friendships.

If we confess our sins, he is faithful and just to forgive us our sins and to cleanse us from all unrighteousness. If we say we have not sinned, we make him a liar, and his word is not in us.

—I JOHN 1:9–10

I talk to God freely about my sins, and He always forgives me. But if I say I haven't messed up, then I am not telling the truth.

Trust

But I trust in you, Lord; I say, "You are my God."

—PSALM 31:14 NIV

Trusting someone means you believe what they say and know they will do what they say they will do. When you trust God, you believe that He is good, that He loves you and will never leave you or forget you. And when you have to do something hard or scary, you can talk to Him about it and remind yourself that He will help you to do what you need to do, no matter how hard it is. Trusting God is wonderful because it helps us be calm and know that everything will be okay.

I'm Ruth. When my husband died, I traveled to Bethlehem with my mother-in-law. It was a sad time. We didn't know what we were going to do, but we trusted God to provide—and He did! I found a job working in the grain fields and eventually married a man named Boaz. You can always trust God!

Check out what the Bible says about trust!

"God's way is perfect. All the Lord's promises prove true. He is a shield for all who look to him for protection."

—2 SAMUEL 22:31 NLT

God always knows the right thing to do, and I believe He will do what is best for me. I trust Him to take care of me at all times!

Trust in him at all times. Pour out your heart to him, for God is our refuge.

—PSALM 62:8 NLT

When I'm scared or worried, I will tell God how I feel and ask Him to help me trust Him more.

Some trust in chariots and some in horses, but we trust in the name of the Lord our God.

—PSALM 20:7

I trust God because He is bigger and better than anyone or anything else in the world!

When I am afraid, I put my trust in you.

—PSALM 56:3

I will ask God to help me feel safe whenever I am scared.

Trust in the Lord with all your heart; do not depend on your own understanding. Seek his will in all you do, and he will show you which path to take.

—PROVERBS 3:5-6 NLT

God knows everything, and He is smarter than everyone in the whole world. I trust Him to show me what's right.

What I Say

Wise words are more valuable
than much gold and many rubies.

PROVERBS 20:15 NLT

Words come from the heart and they are powerful! So, God wants us to choose our words carefully—to share kind and encouraging comments, loving corrections, useful information, and the truth we know from His Word. That way, we will feel good and make others happy with what we say. Sometimes when we're upset, we want to use words to hurt people, but God will always encourage us to tell others that they are loved and special . . . the way we all want to feel inside!

Did You Know?

The whole universe was created through words—the words of God! The book of Genesis says God spoke and there was light. God spoke and there were oceans and dry lands. God spoke and there were stars, animals, and people. Words sure are powerful!

A soft answer turns away wrath, but a harsh word stirs up anger.

—PROVERBS 15:1

My kind words bring peace, but mean words make people angry.

Kind words are like honey— sweet to the soul and healthy for the body.

—PROVERBS 16:24 NLT

Kind words make me feel better and happy!

Don't use foul or abusive language. Let everything you say be good and helpful, so that your words will be an encouragement to those who hear them.

—EPHESIANS 4:29 NLT

I don't use bad words or insults. My words are good and helpful, and they bring encouragement to others.

It is wonderful to say the right thing at the right time!

PROVERBS 15:23 NLT

I am learning to say the right words at the right time.

Set a guard over my mouth, Lord; keep watch over the door of my lips.

—PSALM 141:3 NIV

God helps me watch what I say so I don't hurt others.

Death and life are in the power of the tongue.

—PROVERBS 18:21

I use my words to encourage people, not cause them harm.

What I Think About

**O Lord, you have searched me and known me!
You know when I sit down and when I rise up;
you discern my thoughts from afar.**

—PSALM 139:1-2

Did you know that your thoughts affect your whole life? And did you know that you can choose right now what you are thinking about? Throughout each day, many thoughts come into our heads—good thoughts, silly thoughts, sad thoughts, bad thoughts, mad thoughts. But we can tell each thought that comes our way, "Okay, you can stay" or, "No, you have to go." With God's help, you can make that choice!

Did You Know?

The Bible says to take our thoughts captive. Every time you have a negative, mean, or hurtful thought, imagine grabbing that thought with your hand, locking it in a box, and throwing away the key. When you're in control of your thoughts, it's easier to obey God!

Set your minds on things that are above, not on things that are on earth.

—COLOSSIANS 3:2

I think about all the cool things God is doing around me instead of thinking about things that make me mad or sad.

For to set the mind on the flesh is death, but to set the mind on the Spirit is life and peace.

—ROMANS 8:6

I keep my thoughts on Jesus, and it makes me happy!

Let the Spirit renew your thoughts and attitudes. Put on your new nature, created to be like God— truly righteous and holy.

—EPHESIANS 4:23–24 NLT

God helps me think about good things, and He teaches me to be like Him.

Whatever is true, whatever is honorable, whatever is just, whatever is pure, whatever is lovely, whatever is commendable, if there is any excellence, if there is anything worthy of praise, think about these things.

—PHILIPPIANS 4:8

I choose to think about things that make God smile—being kind, telling the truth, loving others.

We destroy arguments and every lofty opinion raised against the knowledge of God, and take every thought captive to obey Christ.

—2 CORINTHIANS 10:5

I take all my thoughts and give them to God. He shows me what's true.

What Is Faith?

Now faith is confidence in what we hope for and assurance about what we do not see.

—HEBREWS 11:1 NIV

Faith is believing what God says is true, no matter what your thoughts or feelings tell you, and no matter what is happening around you. As God's kids, the most important step of faith we can take is to believe that Jesus is God's Son—and He came to help us! We have faith that God hears us when we pray, that He can make us better when we're sick and for so many other things. Jesus' friend Peter was even able to walk on water because he had faith! (See Matthew 14:22–33.) And if you believe what God says is possible for you—with His help—then you can do the impossible too!

I'm Joshua! God led my people to Jericho, a city with a big wall around it. God promised the city would be ours, but first we had to get through the wall. God told us to march around the wall and blow trumpets for seven days, and on the seventh day, the wall fell down! God is always faithful.

So faith comes from hearing, and hearing through the word of Christ.

—ROMANS 10:17

My faith comes from hearing God's Word . . . about everything Jesus did for us.

"Whoever believes in the Son has eternal life."

—JOHN 3:36

Because of my faith in Jesus, I have been given the gift of life with Jesus forever and ever!

For it is with your heart that you believe and are justified, and it is with your mouth that you profess your faith and are saved.

—ROMANS 10:10 NIV

I know in my heart that Jesus loves me and forgives me, and I tell my friends all about it.

The Bible says a lot about faith. Check it out!

"With man this is impossible, but with God all things are possible."

—MATTHEW 19:26

Whatever I can't do, God can!

"Whoever believes in me will also do the works that I do; and greater works than these will he do, because I am going to the Father."

—JOHN 14:12

I can do amazing things because of my faith in Jesus.

"Be still, and know that I am God!"

PSALM 46:10

I let my mind go quiet, knowing that God is with me.

When I Am Sick

**The Lord sustains him on his sickbed;
in his illness you restore him to full health.**

—PSALM 41:3

Do you remember how you felt the last time you were sick? Sometimes our body hurts and we don't have much energy, and we have to stay home instead of going to school or playing with friends. But God made us, and He knows how to heal us! He wants you to feel your best in every way! When you feel sick, you can ask God to help you and make you feel better.

I was sick for a long time. Nothing made me better! I knew Jesus could heal sick people, so I followed Him one day. When I reached Him, I touched His robe. Jesus knew that someone had touched Him. I said I touched Him because I was sick and needed healing. Jesus healed me right then because of my faith. He can heal you when you're sick too!

By his wounds you have been healed.

—I PETER 2:24

Jesus was hurt so that I could be healed!

Listen carefully to my words. Don't lose sight of them. Let them penetrate deep into your heart, for they bring life to those who find them, and healing to their whole body.

—PROVERBS 4:20–22 NLT

I listen carefully to the words of Jesus. They go to work in my heart and make my whole body healthy.

He sent out his word and healed them, and delivered them from their destruction. Let them thank the Lord for his steadfast love, for his wondrous works to the children of man!

—PSALM 107:20–21

God sent His Son, Jesus, to heal me and forgive me when I sin. I am thankful for His love and the good things He has done!

"You must serve only the Lord your God. If you do, I will bless you with food and water, and I will protect you from illness."

—EXODUS 23:25 NLT

I listen to God and He takes care of me. He provides good food for me and helps me be healthy and strong.

O Lord my God, I cried to you for help, and you have healed me.

—PSALM 30:2

I pray to God when I am sick, and He heals me.

When I'm Lonely

"I love all who love me.
Those who search will surely find me."
—PROVERBS 8:17 NLT

There are so many reasons why we get lonely. Maybe your best friend moved away. Or you're the new kid in class and you're having a hard time making friends. Maybe you feel alone when you come home or wish you could join after-school activities. God wants you to know that He's your forever friend and you can count on Him to comfort you when you're lonely. He can even help you find a brand-new friend!

Let's Talk to God

Jesus, when I'm feeling lonely,
remind me that You are always with me.
I can talk to You as much as I want!
I love You. Amen.

Because of your unfailing love, I can enter your house.

—PSALM 5:7 NLT

Because God loves me more than anything, I can come to Him any time.

See what the Bible says about God being your friend!

"I will not leave you as orphans; I will come to you."

JOHN 14:18

God will never leave me all alone. He will always be there for me.

"Abide in my love."

—JOHN 15:9

I wrap God's love around me like a cozy blanket.

Draw near to God, and he will draw near to you.

—JAMES 4:8

I get closer and closer to God, and He comes closer to me.

"Behold, I am with you always, to the end of the age."

—MATTHEW 28:20

God will always be with me. Always.

He comforts us in all our troubles so that we can comfort others. When they are troubled, we will be able to give them the same comfort God has given us.

—2 CORINTHIANS 1:4 NLT

God comforts me when I'm having a hard time. So, when someone else is going through something tough, I will know how to make them feel better too.

When I'm Mad

Do not lose your temper—it only leads to harm.
—PSALM 37:8 NLT

Remember the last time you or someone you know was mad? How did it make you feel? God wants us to know it's okay to feel mad, but He doesn't want us to act out in ways that hurt others. The truth is, it doesn't do us any good when our feelings get out of control, God can help us get back in control. You can talk to God about what happened and trust Him to work everything out.

My Prayer Today

God, sometimes I feel mad. I know it's not good to keep thinking about angry feelings, so please take away my anger and replace it with happy and grateful thoughts. Amen.

The Bible says a lot about dealing with anger. Check it out!

"But I say to you, Love your enemies and pray for those who persecute you."

—MATTHEW 5:44

I love everyone—even people who don't like me. And I pray for people who hurt me.

Be angry and do not sin; do not let the sun go down on your anger.

—EPHESIANS 4:26

When I'm angry, I don't act out. And I make peace with others before bedtime.

Good sense makes one slow to anger, and it is his glory to overlook an offense.

—PROVERBS 19:11

It doesn't make sense to get angry quickly. And it's good for me to forgive others instead of getting mad.

Let every person be quick to hear, slow to speak, slow to anger.

—JAMES 1:19

I listen first, think before I speak, and I don't get angry.

Beloved, never avenge yourselves, but leave it to the wrath of God, for it is written, "Vengeance is mine, I will repay, says the Lord."

—ROMANS 12:19

I don't try to get even with people who hurt me. I leave it in God's hands, because He promises to make things right.

Who Jesus Made Me to Be

For we are God's handiwork, created in Christ Jesus to do good works, which God prepared in advance for us to do.

—EPHESIANS 2:10 NIV

God made you special—and He has a special plan for your life! He wants you to know how precious you are in His eyes, even if sometimes you may not see what He sees. The truth is, you're so valuable to God that He sent His only Son, Jesus, to give you life with Him forever! He wants you to love the amazing person He created you to be, and to join him in every wonderful adventure He's planned just for you.

Did You Know?

Have you ever tried to count how many hairs you have? It's impossible! But the Bible says God knows the exact number of hairs you have on your head. He made you in His image and He knows you better than anyone!

The Bible says a lot about God's plan for you. Check it out!

God loved us and chose us in Christ to be holy and without fault in his eyes.

—EPHESIANS 1:4 NLT

God loved me and chose me to be His child, and when He looks at me, He is so happy!

I praise you, for I am fearfully and wonderfully made. Wonderful are your works; my soul knows it very well.

—PSALM 139:14

God made me special and I am one of a kind. Everything He does is good!

The Spirit himself bears witness with our spirit that we are children of God.

—ROMANS 8:16

The Holy Spirit tells me that I am a child of God.

Therefore, if anyone is in Christ, the new creation has come: The old has gone, the new is here!

—2 CORINTHIANS 5:17 NIV

When I gave my life to Jesus, I became brand new! The old me went away, and the new me is here!

"Before I formed you in the womb I knew you, and before you were born I consecrated you; I appointed you a prophet to the nations."

—JEREMIAH 1:5

God knew me before I was a baby. He chose me to show the world His love.

Wisdom

**For wisdom is far more valuable than rubies.
Nothing you desire can compare with it.**

—PROVERBS 8:11 NLT

Sometimes it's hard to know the right answer. Maybe you've felt this way when you were taking a test at school or someone wanted you to do something, but you weren't sure if it was a good decision or not. God is awesome because He always knows what is right. And when you follow His wisdom (which means making right choices), you'll always be glad later on, even if it was hard to do it at the time. So anytime you need help making a decision, talk to God and ask Him for help.

Hi! I'm Solomon. I was twenty years old when I became king of Israel. I wanted to make sure the things I did were pleasing to the Lord, so instead of asking for riches or long life like most kings, I asked God for wisdom to rule over His people. God was happy that I didn't ask for selfish gifts, and He granted me wisdom!

Check out what the Bible says about wisdom!

For whoever finds me finds life and receives favor from the Lord.

—PROVERBS 8:35 NIV

God shows me the right things to do, and it makes Him happy when I do them.

If you need wisdom, ask our generous God, and he will give it to you. He will not rebuke you for asking.

—JAMES 1:5 NLT

When I don't know what to do, I will ask God to help me and show me what is right, because He loves me and wants to help me.

Get all the advice and instruction you can, so you will be wise the rest of your life.

—PROVERBS 19:20 NLT

I will learn everything I can from the Bible so I can be wise like God and make the best choices I can.

The wise inherit honor, but fools are put to shame!

—PROVERBS 3:35 NLT

I will do what God says is right so I am not sad about the choices I make.

Fear of the Lord is the foundation of true wisdom. All who obey his commandments will grow in wisdom.

—PSALM 111:10 NLT

I love God and want to do what is right because it will help me be wise like Him and make better choices my whole life!

A Closing Note

God loves you so much! He wants you to remember this every single day. That's why He gave us His Word, the Bible. When we read the Bible, we learn more and more about God and how we can make the best choices we can so we can be more like Him!

Some days it's easy to be happy and to feel thankful for God's love and everything He does for us. And other days, when we feel sad or mad, it's hard to think about how good God is. But when we read the Bible and think about what it says, it helps us have a better day—whether we're already happy or not. And there's nothing better than talking to God about our day and knowing He's right there with us!

So let's thank God for being so good and loving us so much!

God, thank You so much for loving me
and showing me how special I am to You.
Thank You for giving me the Bible
so I can learn about You and how
to do good things that help others.
I'm very glad that You are with me
all the time, wherever I go.
Thank You for being my best friend.
I love You, God!
Amen.